The Recruiter is Your Friend

The Recruiter is Your Friend

◆

This Ain't Your Granddaddy's Job Search

Kristen M. Hallows, BBA

iUniverse, Inc.

New York Lincoln Shanghai

The Recruiter is Your Friend
This Ain't Your Granddaddy's Job Search

iUniverse books may be ordered through booksellers or by contacting:

iUniverse
2021 Pine Lake Road, Suite 100
Lincoln, NE 68512
www.iuniverse.com
1-800-Authors (1-800-288-4677)

ISBN-13: 978-0-595-41896-1 (pbk)
ISBN-13: 978-0-595-86244-3 (ebk)
ISBN-10: 0-595-41896-1 (pbk)
ISBN-10: 0-595-86244-6 (ebk)

Printed in the United States of America

Contents

Foreword . . . . *vii*

Chapter 1   What You Need to Know 1

Chapter 2   Change Your Perspective and Your Attitude
                    While You're At It 15

Chapter 3   Résumé Writing and Beyond 19

Chapter 4   Why Recruiters Make Sense 26

Chapter 5   Job Searching in the Future 35

References *53*

Foreword

Even if you have never dreamed of being a CEO, you can be one right now. Managing and directing your job search campaign can be just as challenging and demanding as running a business.

Speaking of which, you do not have to wait or invest lots of money to start a side business that fuels your creative energy and provides light at the end of the tunnel while you decide what to do with your career. While there are some insightful, interesting ones out there, I do not believe that you can decide what to do with your life by taking a personality test. This is something that only you can decide after exposing yourself to a wide variety of stimuli—and possibly a vacation here and there.

At times you may feel like a trapped animal, but you have control over your career. I guarantee you that no one will ever care about your future as much as you do. So it only makes sense for you to be the CEO.

But don't get comfortable in the plush corner office yet. If you do not perform, you could get ousted. Like any great CEO, you must know when to take the next step, and you must decide which relationships are worth building. Your job search campaign does not have to be stressful or inefficient. I truly hope that this book will provide you with the inspiration to develop *your* career.

1

What You Need to Know

The Job Search is Lined with Potholes...and Some Contain Explosives

Launching and managing a job search campaign can be as time consuming and expensive as starting and running a business. I am confident, though, that those who are successful at either one will tell you that all of the hard work was worth it.

When the economy is doing well and unemployment is down, people may begin a job search in reaction to less competition. Conversely, when more people are unemployed, fewer people may launch a job search campaign because they are scared of being crushed by the competition. I am willing to bet that almost all small business owners will advise you not to let your competition prevent you from starting your business. The same is true for starting your job search.

The purpose of this first chapter is to educate you, one of today's job seekers. With more and more people competing for fewer and fewer jobs, competition *is* tough. However, armed with the right knowledge and strategies, your efforts will pay off.

One Thing You Can Do Right *Now*

Stop applying for positions that are advertised. Do not waste one more second perusing the Sunday paper. I am referring to Internet job boards as well as newspapers.

I love the Internet. It has enabled me to meet and interact with people all over the world. Most small businesses have their first dollar framed. I framed my first PayPal invoice because my very first customer paid me via email. I strongly suggest you use the Internet to buy cell phones and find a veterinarian, but I urge you to be cautious when using it to find something as important as your next career move!

If you have ever posted a résumé on a major Internet job board, you have probably been a victim of what some call the "shotgun method" or "blasting." I will discuss the safety concerns later, but first let me point out why it is not a good idea for job seekers OR recruiters to practice this in any way—ever.

When you post a résumé on a job board and get responses as early as the next day, you feel pretty good about it. Then you realize that what are clogging up your inbox are merely form emails inviting you to work for a life insurance company or another organization that is totally unrelated to your career goal. This does not make you feel special, does it?

From a recruiter's point of view, blasting is no fun, either. As they eagerly sort through responses to their job advertisements, they begin to wonder if the vast majority of applicants even read the descriptions! People just want jobs, and some believe that if they apply for enough positions, eventually they will get one.

Quantity displaces quality. Both the job seeker and the recruiter receive too many unqualified responses. This is undoubtedly the most frustrating aspect of advertised job postings for both parties.

You may have heard that the most sought after jobs are not posted. This is true for a number of reasons. By the time you see a job advertised, the company may intend to offer the job to another candidate. The job could be posted simply to satisfy legal requirements. If you have ever applied for a job and received a letter shortly thereafter informing you that another candidate has been chosen, this is likely the reason.

Every once in awhile you come across a job description, and you think that only one or two people in the entire world could meet those requirements. This is what I call the Impossible Job Description Problem. It is also an example of a company posting a job "just to post it," with an offer pending to someone else the entire time it is advertised.

Another possibility is that someone simply neglected to take the posting down after the job was filled. You are left wondering why you never got the opportunity to interview! Also, you completely wasted your time.

Wait, There's More

If an employer does not want a current employee to know that he or she is being replaced, why would the employer post the job for the world to see? In a situation like this, the employer would talk to a recruiter, and the search would be done confidentially.

Consider this as well. For the same reason the Internet has become a popular place to look for jobs and everything else, top talent (that's you) does not want to submit résumés or post messages on discussion boards because some are afraid their current employers will somehow find out. This is highly possible! The information depot that is the Internet has made the world a very small place.

So job seekers *and* employers want to search confidentially. For more observations on the future of the job search process, please be sure to read Chapter Five.

You could also be applying for a job that does not exist. Companies advertising a job for a secretary or administrative assistant could really be looking for management candidates. During interviews, they ask the secretaries about their bosses! If they need lenders, they could advertise a lending assistant position. The applicants are asked about the best lenders for whom they have ever worked. These candidates believe they are being interviewed for a genuine position, yet the employers never intended to hire them. This is beyond bad karma…this is illegal. However, it does happen.

I have also heard of companies advertising a fictitious job simply to gather résumés for the future, which is frustrating because there is a legal way to approach this. It *is* legal to post a job even if the company does not have an immediate need. If this is the case, there should be a disclaimer such as "we do not have specific positions open at this time."

Some postings may be legitimate, but this book is not for employers. It is for you. Do you really want to risk applying for a job that is unavailable or nonexistent? Time is a nonrenewable resource.

This is not including the dishonest things that have been done by unprofessional recruiters. I will expand on this in a later chapter.

Use the Internet to Build Your Network (Do Not Use It to Look for Jobs)

Looking for anything on the Internet can be an overwhelming experience due to the vast amount of information available. But the Internet is quite possibly the best, most comprehensive tool that is available to you at little or no cost.

There are two types of Internet job hunter. Your type will likely determine how successful you are at finding the job you seek.

Type A uses the Internet to look for job advertisements, and then she applies for positions by following each post's instructions. This type tends to be frustrated and disillusioned with the entire process because he or she experiences the vicious cycle described on the back cover.

Type B uses the Internet as a networking tool. She joins and subscribes to as many networking sites, discussion groups, forums and blogs as possible. This person builds relationships and obtains job leads and contact information for key decision makers through her network of friends and colleagues.

You can probably imagine which one is more likely to find a job. This is exactly the problem: type As use the Internet to find jobs when they should be using the Internet to network, which leads to the jobs they want.

Let me use myself as an example. I subscribe to many daily email newsletters that provide useful advice and contact information for individuals who can provide support and recommendations. Most are completely free of charge. I belong to WorldWIT, StartupNation, Shared Vision Network and the Electronic Recruiter Exchange. I subscribe to the Coaching Compass newsletter from Coach Training Alliance and the Business Success newsletter from Arca Max Publishing. I also subscribe to The Wall Street Journal. If you would like more information about any of these organizations, do not hesitate to contact me.

I believe MySpace, Facebook, LinkedIn and other social networking sites can be helpful in establishing an online presence and building relationships. Plus, recruiters have been known to review sites like these in the eternal search for candidates. You *can* use your social networking page to promote yourself; however, design its content carefully.

To Post or Not to Post…That is Definitely the Question

Certainly you have heard about companies deciding not to hire applicants after finding photos of them passed out at a party or using drugs on the Internet. I still have not figured out why drunken photos are so popular. I thought it was a college thing, but I have older friends who still have them proudly displayed on their pages. I thought I read somewhere *not* to have a drink in your hand in pictures!

Here is a useful piece of information for people of any age. According to Shannon Ross, an attorney for the National Association of Personnel Services (NAPS), "an employer *can* use information it finds on a Web site to disqualify a candidate" (Shannon Ross, personal communication, October 9, 2006). You can Google your date, so why not Google a potential employee? My advice has always been to keep it professional just in case your prospective employer, your boyfriend or your grandmother Googles your name.

Most likely, if an employer decides not to hire you after digging up information about you on the Internet, you will never know. You just will not get an interview or a job offer. I read a story about a college student who not so mysteriously started getting interviews once he took down an essay he wrote titled "Lying Your Way to the Top" (Finder, 2006, ¶ 19).

If you *are* given a reason, it will most likely be something other than the real reason. This is exactly why you should not tell a prospective employer you are pregnant during an interview. It is illegal to discriminate based on this, but you will probably never know the *real* reason you were not hired.

If you post it on the Internet, you are responsible for the consequences.

Networking: Still the Best Way to Find a Job!

Your name could come up at a PDA Party.

PDA Parties, also known as Rolodex Parties, are organized gatherings where everyone divulges the names of top performers from other companies they know. Why would people want to do this? Usually they are lured by free lunch. Plus, they say the energy is contagious, and everyone is happy to do her part.

The main idea is the top talent at other companies is somehow connected to the best people in your own firm. The people whose names are given at the party could be targeted by recruiters in the future (Sullivan, 2006, ¶ 2-8). This is a much better way to obtain good information than holding interviews for positions that do not exist—and legal, too!

You could be discovered while sipping beverages with colleagues.

Scared to be seen with colleagues after hours? Get over it. You may be missing opportunities to be found by recruiters.

I remember being reprimanded by a co-worker for allowing my ID badge to hang from my bag when we met at a sports bar. He mumbled something about the image of the office. At that time, I was looking for another job, and I should have displayed it more prominently!

Since then, I have learned my lesson about the networking potential of bars. My husband and I recently met a friend at a bar, and I only brought my ID and a credit card. I quickly regretted that decision. I missed two separate opportunities to distribute a few business cards. The friend we met had a brother who had been laid off, and another person at the bar was looking for a new job. I told them a little about what I do, but with loud music and alcohol, it becomes more difficult to remember even a catchy name like "jobyoudeserve.com."

This brings me to another point. You are a professional, correct? Why shouldn't you have business cards? They are fun to design, and they make people want to contact you more than a handwritten number on a crumpled-up napkin or piece of paper. The moral of the story is that you never know who you will meet wherever you go. So next time your friends want to go out on a Friday night and all you want to do is go to bed early, go out with them! Promise yourself you will only stay for an hour, and see what happens.

Good recruiters know where their targets are likely to hang out. Bars and other work-related social gatherings are prime places. So are alumni reunions, charity events and wine festivals (Sullivan, 2006, ¶ 7). Next time you observe a bunch of people dressed in business casual attire with ID badges hanging from their belts, do not be surprised if the man or woman talking with one of them is a recruiter.

That annual conference or development day may be good for your career.

Sales conferences and regional meetings are other places where aggressive recruiters tend to instigate battles in the war for talent. Usually companies send only their best and brightest to these events. Furthermore, they present them with trophies, plaques, t-shirts and other awards that indicate they are top performers (Sullivan, 2006, ¶ 5). It is like putting a spotlight on a buffalo for a group of lions…in a good way.

You can network wherever you go.

Anyone you come into contact with can join your network. Tell your stylist, your massage therapist and even your auto mechanic. You never know who will hear you at the right time. Karen Mattonen of ACS Search in San Diego, California told me an interesting story that proves this point perfectly. One of her first placements came shortly after she launched her recruiting business. She was still trying to decide on a specialization, and she was discussing this with her husband one night at a restaurant. Someone at a table nearby overheard her conversation. He went to his car, retrieved his résumé, and handed it to Karen saying she should specialize in the real estate industry. She decided to specialize in construction, but they were able to help each other.

I do not recommend telling every stranger you meet; however, in the US, "what do you do?" is a frequently asked question. A friend of mine, who is a nurse, was visiting the pool in her neighborhood recently. She heard someone talking about an open position at a local hospital, and my friend now works for this hospital.

Networking is vital to job seekers *and* business owners. Let me use my cross-promoting relationship with a recruiter as an example. When he has a candidate who needs résumé assistance, he refers her to me because I am a professional résumé writer and career coach. When I have a client who needs help finding a job, I refer her to the recruiter (more on this in Chapter Four).

This can work for you, too. Do you have a friend or family member who is employed by a company you would like to work for? Instead of going to the company's Web site, ask your friend or family member about the company's hiring needs. This person may know of an available or soon to be available position before other people in the company know about it!

Depending on your relationship with your friend or family member, she may even recommend you for a position. This may not be an ongoing partnership, but you will probably find an opportunity to help someone else. Current employees may be asked to refer new employees more often in the future (e.g., PDA parties).

I have found repeatedly that if I want referrals, all I have to do is give referrals whenever possible. Mention a friend or business partner, and she will do the same for you. Dave Liniger, co-founder and chairman of RE/MAX International, said, "To be successful, you can't show up to the potluck with just a fork." Of course, if you are dealing with someone who always expects something in return (they are called quid pro quo networkers), find a new partner.

Do not be afraid to tell others that you are actively looking for a job. You will be surprised at how many people want to help.

2

Change Your Perspective and Your Attitude While You're At It

XYZ Company, Will You Go Out With Me?

I have always found it easy to view the employee/employer relationship similar to a dating relationship. People put up with things from their employers that they would *never* tolerate from their partners.

There is one key difference, you say. Your main source of income is not your spouse or boy/girlfriend. He or she does not pay for the majority of your health insurance like a typical employer does. But how is someone who is hanging on to his hellish job simply because it pays the mortgage any different from someone who stays in a relationship only because his house constantly looks like a page out of a Williams Sonoma catalog? In both cases, something is clearly wrong...but the person is unwilling or unable to make the change(s) necessary to correct the situation!

I am sure you have heard the job interview is as much for you as it is for the employer. Sounds good, right? But how many people approach an interview with this in mind? Usually all we can think about is how we wish we could relax! Most of us go into a job interview hoping the employer will like us and eventually hire us. In other words, we tend to not approach the situation with the attitude of an equal. Even a slight lack of confidence will cause you to see the employer as above you or more powerful than you. At that point, it's all about the employer. What about you? What do *you* want in an employer? In a career? You would never approach a relationship this way!

When you think of an interview as an opportunity to interview the employer and evaluate it as *your potential employer*, your confidence increases a little, doesn't it? You start to find the confidence to ask important questions, which makes you appear interested, which is attractive to an employer. This sounds like a cycle I can live with!

But, you say, when money is involved, everything changes. Does it? If you truly need a job to pay the bills until you establish your criteria for a *career*, my advice is to visit a staffing agency. No, these are not dream jobs, but…they pay the bills.

Once money is no longer an immediate issue, you can focus on determining exactly what *you* want. Do not interview just to interview. Few things make me cringe more than when I hear someone say, "I'll take any job." You would not waste your time in a relationship with someone you see no future with, correct?

Your Bad Attitude Does Not Attract Success

When I am in a bad mood, no one can talk me down from it. Sound familiar? Like my husband says, "blowing sunshine up your butt" only makes you more upset. However, even if you do not believe in karma, you know that being nice to people pays dividends. And when you are obviously in a bad mood, at best you will not attract friends, and at worst you will end up in the elevator with a happy delivery guy you just want to choke!

As a career coach, one of the best things I can do to build my business is establish relationships. I do this by going out and meeting people in coffee shops, in discussion groups and in virtually all other social situations. You are no different. Being approachable and reaching out to people may be difficult when things are not turning out the way you planned, but

I dare you to do it anyway. Focus on someone else's challenges, and you may drastically change the direction *your* day is going. You might pick up a friend, a customer or even a business partner!

3

Résumé Writing and Beyond

There are many lessons to be learned from sales. Have you ever heard that people do not like to be sold to, but they love to buy? Your résumé should "sell" you so well that its reader will want to meet you even if there is no need for someone with your skill set.

No matter whose desk your résumé lands on, it must clearly communicate your value. How is your recruiter going to portray you as an ideal candidate if she is not aware of *all* of your major selling points?

Maybe I should add a note about being honest with your résumé writer, too! I am not trying to promote myself, but I must say something about a professionally written résumé. If created exclusively for you with all necessary information, there is nothing better to promote you and your abilities. Think of it as your own sales brochure.

When you talk about your job search campaign, think of every conversation as a practice interview. Practice selling yourself. Think like a deeply-involved CEO who does a lot of networking and selling. Do not be afraid to describe your most significant achievements and what you have to offer.

Determine What is Relevant

A one size fits all résumé is pointless because it is ineffective. If you have a very diverse background, include all of your achievements, but do not be afraid to list your current position somewhere on the second page if it is totally unrelated to your career objective.

The reverse chronological format is still the best to use when describing professional experience, but who said your current job has to be listed first? If you are working as a temp answering telephones but your real passion lies in animal science, the temp job is not going to grab a hiring manager's attention.

However, while you do not have to list your current position first, do not deviate from the reverse chronological format by listing your work experience in any way other than most recent to oldest. Hiring managers generally like to see what you have done where and when. Any other format may make them suspect you are hiding something such as lack of experience or unstable job history.

Even if your related experience is volunteer work or happened a few years ago, list it first. Of course, if your experience is technical in nature, make sure to communicate how you have kept your skills current. This is especially true for people over 40. Place your most significant selling points in the top half of the first page.

It is extremely important for your résumé to clearly and quickly explain exactly why you should be granted an interview. If the reader has to figure it out, she will not take the time to do so. This is not a treasure hunt. If your most important achievements are saved for last, most likely the reader will not get far enough to learn about them.

Design *Your* Advertisement

Designing a résumé is not much different from creating an impressive, attention-grabbing advertisement for potential customers. Why can't you have a SWOT analysis or pie chart in the middle of the first page? Why shouldn't you include a sample of your work as an appendix?

I recently picked up a novel by an author who is a "Winner of the National Book Award." Why couldn't you mention loud and clear that you are a "Winner of the Employee of the Quarter Award?" If it is true, why not include it under your name?

Ban Objective Statements

With all due respect, no hiring manager cares about what *you* want. Do you want to work for a growing company? Do you desire to sharpen your communication and leadership skills? So what? Most likely the two most important things going through a hiring authority's mind are the following:

- "What can you do for my company?"
- "Will hiring you make me look good?"

People do not refer or hire others without carefully considering that decision because the people they refer or hire have the potential to make them look really good...or really bad. Give the reader something to feel confident about.

Turn your objective statement into a professional summary that proves why anyone with the privilege of reviewing your résumé should meet you—even if there are no immediate hiring needs.

Use the top "résumé real estate" as an opportunity to give the reader a reason and a desire to read further.

Make a list of your top ten areas of expertise. Then, narrow that list down to the top three. These three areas should definitely be included near the top of page one. The remaining seven should also be prominently listed somewhere in the top half of the first page.

Résumé writing is an intricate topic for another book, but below is a basic example of the opening of an attention-grabbing résumé. Keep in mind that résumés, like people and businesses and Web sites, are constantly evolving. Do not forget to make updates!

KRISTEN M. HALLOWS, BBA

Post Office Box 385 Columbus, Ohio 43026

877-832-5400 (toll-free) 614-589-8720 (local)

khallows@jobyoudeserve.com www.jobyoudeserve.com

"…exemplary service and professionalism…"

RÉSUMÉ STRATEGIST AND CAREER COACH

Communications professional with demonstrated analytical skills, personal ingenuity and ability to motivate others. Proven capacity to produce extremely high quality work in short periods of time.

I strongly suggest integrating testimonials from clients, supervisors and/or colleagues. If you have a copy of a letter of recommendation, look for key quotes to include. After all, this is *your* advertisement that will proclaim what you are capable of!

"Kristen's written papers were a joy to read...they were clear, to the point and well documented...she is an articulate person who can clearly express her thoughts."
—William N. D'Onofrio, MBA, CPA

Should I Worry About Writing a Cover Letter?

There are many different opinions on how much cover letters matter. It seems to depend on the person viewing your documents.

I think the cover letter should be considered an opportunity to make the reader want to review your résumé and any attachments. It is a business letter that should be given thought and attention. Keep it simple, and do not overuse the thesaurus. There are people out there who think big, impressive words will make them sound more intelligent or important. In reality, all this usually does is confuse the reader. Do not force the reader to decipher your point. If you do, your work will end up in the recycle bin very quickly.

If the recipient never reads your cover letter, that is fine because your résumé should stand on its own. At least you will be prepared in case your documents land on the desk of a hiring manager who happens to read cover letters.

4

Why Recruiters Make Sense

When you need groceries, you go to a grocery store. When you need pet supplies, you go to a pet supply store. When you need a new job, where do you go?

Unfortunately, jobs cannot be so easily obtained, but recruiters can provide a more direct path to your next employer.

Recruiters' clients are employers. They are paid to find qualified candidates to fill their clients' empty positions. *You* are what recruiters need to satisfy their clients. Each one may not always be able to help you, but ideally your relationship with a recruiter will be mutually beneficial.

The Good, The Bad and The Heinous

Though I highly recommend recruiters, I would like job seekers to be informed. Recruiters are not regulated like doctors or lawyers. This means you should research your recruiter even more thoroughly than you would a medical or legal professional. When you have found a recruiter who matches you with a rewarding job that provides you with years of fulfillment, you will be glad you spent a little time doing your research.

Do not partner with just any recruiter! The recruiting industry is a lot like the Internet. There are plenty of excellent resources out there, but there are also a great deal of people and places you should avoid. Many recruiters are honest, reputable and professional. Unfortunately, some are inconsiderate, disrespectful criminals.

Before I explain how to find and establish a dating relationship with your recruiter, let me thoroughly describe some potential traps to be aware of during your search. To provide a comprehensive list, I consulted with Karen Mattonen.

Who is Looking at Your Résumé?

It is amazing how many people "blast" their résumés all over the Internet. When I mention "blasting," I am referring to posting your résumé on Internet job boards as well as sending your résumé to random recruiters. Believe it or not, recruiters receive résumés that include Social Security numbers and pictures of the candidates! Once I heard about a candidate who submitted copies of his entire medical history with his résumé. Do you want your personal information to be available to everyone including dishonest recruiters and identity thieves? No one expects to become a victim of identity theft as a result of looking for a new job, but it is possible.

This is a true story. A recruiter once found a job seeker's résumé on Monster.com, and he or she submitted the résumé without the candidate's permission. The applicant was granted an interview and filled out an application ahead of time. Sound familiar? The organization turned out to be illegitimate, and the information obtained from the forms was used to commit identity theft.

In addition to being careful where you post your résumé, also be mindful of whose Web site to which you submit your résumé. One poor soul visited a Web site that he thought belonged to a reputable investment company. The Web site's name was misspelled, but it was close enough that he did not notice the error. He received an email notifying him that the hiring manager was interested, and a background check would be necessary. The email asked for information such as a password and his mother's maiden name. This person thought he was speaking with a company representative. Well, the fraudulent company took his information, and soon the victim discovered that his checking account had been emptied. These criminals are smart. They know that most people use the same password for multiple accounts.

Identity theft is very real, but it should not be a risk if you are working with a trustworthy recruiter!

How Can I Find the Right Recruiter?

The following was adapted from Karen Mattonen's list of candidate rights.

1. Research!

    You would research your doctor or lawyer, so please carefully research your recruiter. Karen strongly recommends finding a recruiter who specializes in your target industry. You could start by using Google or another search engine. For example, search for "medical recruiter," "pharmaceutical recruiter," or "hvac recruiter." From there, you can shop around by location. Also, ask your friends and family whom they use.

    Check out professional associations such as the National Association of Personnel Services (www.recruitinglife.com), the American Staffing Association (www.americanstaffing.net), and the Kennedy Association (www.kennedyinfo.com). Your state may have an association; for example, California has the California Staffing Association. Contact your local chamber of commerce, small business association or Better Business Bureau. For a list of regional associations, go to www.damianservices.com/ sub_why_ina.asp.

2. Maintain communication.

This is a big one. It is important to talk to your recruiter. Let this person know who you are, why you are looking, your goals and needs, etc. Try to find out as early as possible if she is looking for someone with your skill set. Ask what to expect and what you need to do as a candidate.

Be honest, but not too honest. Some recruiters are trying to find candidates with or without regard for the people they affect along the way. Recruiters need information like work history, salary information, your reason for leaving, etc. But do not share the names of companies with which you are interviewing. If you are speaking with an unethical recruiter, she may submit her best candidates to those companies as soon as you hang up the phone or leave the office

(Karen Mattonen, personal communication, September 22, 2006).

Look for recruiters (and résumé writers) who belong to at least one professional organization. Professionals who are members in good standing of one or more of these organizations have demonstrated commitment to their industries. I personally believe that continuing education is extremely important, and my professional association helps me keep my skills current by offering teleconferences and the ability to connect with colleagues.

The Recruiter is Your Friend

Unfortunately, few recruiters have enough time to develop a relationship with their clients, the employers. This means they may not fully understand real job needs. In my opinion, a good recruiter is one who promptly returns your phone calls and email messages. One who does not do this consistently must be overwhelmed with obligations, and she may not be able to give you the attention you deserve.

A recruiter may be able to help you get around the Impossible Job Description Problem described in Chapter One. When you find a job advertisement that asks for qualifications that only one in five thousand people have, it makes you wonder who on earth applies for these positions. It is frustrating when you discover a job you are very interested in that asks for one or two more years of experience than you currently have.

This is where a recruiter may be able to open doors for you. A recruiter who works in partnership with hiring managers may be able to negotiate. For example, if a manager tells the recruiter that the candidate must have three years of experience in a healthcare setting, the recruiter can ask, "Would you be willing to meet someone who can do the job with two years of experience in a healthcare setting?"

This is one reason why it is *so* important for your résumé to highlight accomplishments even more than education or work experience. Just as recruiters should not post boring job descriptions, you should not have a typical résumé. Tell your recruiter about major projects, awards and glowing performance reviews. This information will help her communicate that you are capable of accomplishing the work the employer needs to have done.

A good recruiter who is familiar with the job should be able to poke holes in nonsensical, inflexible requirements. When you know what your client needs, you can better sell your product. For example, if your recruiter has a thorough understanding of the job and the candidate, she should be able to convince the employer that just because you are one year short of the required three years of experience in a healthcare setting, you have been consistently recognized for your ability to perform the job duties in question.

If you fall short of the requirements listed in job advertisements, you may try to explain it in your cover letter. This is admirable, but in a tight job market, all I can say is "good luck." Working with a recruiter, you are more likely to get the attention you need from a hiring manager.

Other Things You Can Do *Now*

Get a Web site. Start a blog. Companies do it. CEOs themselves do it. Why shouldn't you do it to promote your own brand awareness? If you are at your energy-sapping, life-draining job right now, you can start a side business to give you renewed energy and determination. Become a consultant. Offer your services on your Web site. Laws vary by state, but depending on the product or service you offer, the only thing you may want to do beforehand is register your business name with your secretary of state's office.

If your blog attracts enough visitors, you may eventually be approached by advertisers. People *will* stumble across your blog while using a major search engine. Depending on the diversity of your content, people may find your blog by accident. We all have experienced this. You are searching for more information about something, and you find a link to a discussion group or blog you have never heard of before. Blogs are indexed through search engines like other Web pages. The number one excuse for not blogging is "I don't have enough time." This is not a good excuse because if you can spare half an hour every other day, you can blog.

Blogging is also a great way to network, especially if your blog becomes very popular. There are thousands of blogs out there, but do not let that stop you. You never know who might visit or post a comment.

5

Job Searching in the Future

Searching Confidentially

Job seekers, recruiters and employers hate unqualified responses that waste time and energy. They also despise having their plans unexpectedly discovered by the one person from whom they were supposed to be kept secret! When you are looking for another job, you probably do not want your boss to find out. When you would like to replace an employee, you most likely do not want her to know until you have found a suitable replacement.

As privacy becomes more of an issue for both sides of the hiring equation, I expect more programs like QuietAgent.com (2006) to be developed. I am in no way affiliated with or compensated by this organization, but I am mentioning it because I think it provides a glimpse into the future.

Even happily employed people are always looking for a better opportunity. Recruiters frequently discuss gaining the interest of passive candidates. These are people who are not actively seeking another position but could be receptive to a better offer if one came along. Aggressive recruiters often prefer to target these people because people who are not actively looking are much more attractive than desperate people whose résumés have been "blasted" all over the Internet.

So what is a professional to do if she does not want certain people to know she is looking for another job? Quiet Agent is an interesting concept. In addition to describing yourself in your own words, you can explain your experience using a standard set of skills and experience developed by the US Department of Labor. This encourages objectivity instead of subjectivity, which occurs when individual employers determine job requirements.

Employers can then sort through a ranked list of matches and decide which candidates they wish to invite. When a job seeker receives an invitation, she can decline the invitation and remain anonymous or accept the invitation and reveal private information to specific employers.

Quiet Agent seems to eliminate the "job search" as we know it. There is no searching. Of course, everyone must still be reasonable and honest. If your expectations are too high, you may never receive an invitation from an employer. Conversely, some job seekers do not care about privacy. In fact, some may want their superiors to know they are looking elsewhere, and that is fine, too. I am certain that there is a recruiter out there who would love to present you to a prospective employer.

What Type of Player are You?

Recruiters are almost always trying to find top talent. These top performers are referred to as A players. They are the employees who work 60 or more hours a week and tend to have higher turnover. This is not entirely due to stress. These people are constantly looking for a better offer, and most of the time there is a recruiter from a competing company at the door to offer them one.

An organization primarily consists of B players, but please do not think they are inferior in any way. B players are the employees who have a life outside of work. Their careers are important, but so are their families and other interests. Some B players are former A players who decided to make time for other things in life. A players may have the ideas, but B players are the ones who execute those ideas. Without B players, fantastic ideas would never materialize.

Far fewer jobs exist for A players than for B players. The war for talent will always be about recruiting the "best," but I believe that in the future, more emphasis will be placed on finding and attracting B players. Companies need to find dependable people who will stick around for awhile.

The Coming Labor Shortage

I am sure you have heard about the baby boomers' exodus from the workforce that will be occurring in the next few years (assuming "retirement age" is 66, the first boomers should be retiring around 2012). I am also certain you have heard about the predicted healthcare shortage, especially in nursing. These are surely issues that will affect the labor market; however, I do not think they deserve all of the attention they are getting.

I believe a main reason for today's nursing shortage is that so many baby boomers chose nursing, and now they are looking at retirement en masse. Further, this generation tended to stay with an employer for decades.

Younger generations have different work habits and attitudes toward work. Generations X and Y change jobs and careers like they change their clothes. They care very much about their careers, but they also have personal lives that are more important. Does this sound familiar? These people are the B players recruiters will be looking for.

Some people believe that outsourcing, immigration, increased productivity ("doing more with less") and delayed retirements will alleviate a potential labor shortage. For the following reasons, I strongly disagree:

- Many people have learned from experience that out-sourcing is *not* a viable option. Quite simply, hassles like language barriers and cultural differences are not worth the lower cost.

- In the past, the US has turned to immigration to obtain needed workers. But times have changed. The experts in math and science we need may choose to stay in their native countries because these countries are rapidly developing.

- We all know that "doing more with less" tends to have negative consequences. People eventually become less productive, unhappy and more likely to seek better employment.

- The concept of delayed retirement almost sounds like a death sentence. Unless you truly enjoy your career, you are not going to want to stick around. I know a lot of people who dream about the day they can retire. In all seriousness, this is only a temporary solution. These delayed retirees can only work for so long. Plus, they are not likely to want to work 40 or more hours a week like their younger colleagues.

Other factors to consider are economic growth and lack of qualified workers. A serious labor shortage can inhibit economic growth. We have plenty of people but not enough qualified workers. Top executives with experience running successful businesses in the US are being targeted by recruiters in other countries, and experts from other countries are staying at home instead of coming to the US. Why? Because the US is not as attractive as it used to be. Other countries are developing and now have more to offer. They are allowing these people to have a great career and be closer to their families.

When we have a lack of engineers, for example, we find the talent we need in other countries such as India. What happens when India becomes more developed and Indian engineers do not want to leave their families? Then recruiters in the US will have to compete with aggressive recruiters in other countries.

The war for talent will never truly end. Separating the qualified workers from the rest will always be a top priority. I urge people to take relevant courses, even if your major is undecided. Of course, one or two classes will not provide you with a tremendous amount of preparation, but taking classes you normally would not be interested in may help you choose a rewarding career path.

I once heard about a lawyer who works as a registered nurse on the weekends. I am not suggesting that you do this, but one word you could use to describe her is "prepared." Think of it as diversifying your portfolio. At this time, it is safe to say that there is more of a demand for nurses than for lawyers. But with time, this scenario may change.

A former co-worker whose job was to deliver the mail appeared to have no marketable skills. Eventually I found out that he was also a carpenter. He built wood fences for a mutual friend, and his work was very impressive. I commented that he should start a business, and I was told that he already had a side business. Good for him!

Only you can decide what you are truly passionate about. I strongly suggest you market your abilities. Why not start a side business? If you are currently dissatisfied in your job, do not put your life on hold until you find another job.

I have a friend who works in a typical office environment. It is one of those places where creativity goes to die. She is very artistic and enjoys creating children's books, puzzles and games. I think she would be very successful if she ever started doing this professionally.

More Information to Ponder

The coming labor shortage, no matter how ominous you expect it will be, is a quality vs. quantity issue. The problem will not be a lack of workers. It will be a lack of *qualified* workers! My main point here is that if your primary selling point is a bachelor's degree, you can probably expect a long job search.

I retrieved the following information from The Princeton Review and an article by Erin Burt (2006). Can you locate the discrepancy in the table below?

Most Popular College Majors	Top Ten Fastest-Growing Jobs
1. Business administration and management	1. **Network systems & data communication analyst**
2. Psychology	2. Physician assistant
3. Elementary education	3. **Computer applications software engineer**
4. Biology	4. **Computer systems software engineer**
5. Nursing	5. Network and computer systems administrator
6. Education	6. **Database administrator**
7. English	7. Physical therapist
8. Communications	8. Medical scientist
9. **Computer science**	9. Occupational therapist
10. Political science	10. College instructor

To qualify for the number one, three, four and six fastest-growing jobs, you must major in the second *least* popular area, which is computer science. Most of the others require a strong undergraduate foundation in areas like biology and chemistry. Psychology and business majors will have to obtain additional training if they want to enter these growing fields.

I am not implying that you should choose a major based solely on its ability to get you a job after graduation. I am, however, inviting you to plan very carefully. What are you going to *do* with that degree in business or psychology? Because more people now have four-year degrees, simply having the degree will not set you apart.

Your ability to find a fulfilling career depends on other factors. In the sea of job seekers, what sets you apart? Are you multilingual? Do you have considerable work and/or volunteer experience in your chosen field? If you answer yes to at least one of these questions, congratulations! You have set yourself apart from those who drifted through college believing that their degrees would be all they need to land a great job.

Colleges and universities are partially to blame for misinformed consumers. Their advertisements imply or clearly state that you will not advance in your career without the degree program they offer. Anyone who has ever been employed should recognize such a concept as false. People are promoted and recognized because they produce results—not simply because they earn a degree! Sometimes people are promoted purely because of their social or political connections, but this is something we cannot control.

If you expect to be promoted once you earn your advanced degree, do yourself a favor and lower your expectations. Colleges and universities want you to believe that you will not succeed without their program, but you must remember that they are businesses, too. They are simply trying to sell their product or service just like any other for-profit organization.

I hate to say this, but career services offices at most colleges are ineffective at best. They seem to consist of well-meaning people who say things most students already know. They hand them mass-produced booklets on résumé and cover letter writing and send them on their way.

This is why I encourage job seekers at any stage in their careers to take personal responsibility for their future successes. No one on this earth cares more about your future than you do. Therefore, you must take action right now. Make yourself marketable by learning and being exposed to as much as possible.

Balanced "Diet"

Compare your résumé to a balanced meal on a plate. Think of the chicken breast as your professional employment (work history). The mashed potatoes represent your extra projects at work, side business, volunteer and/or intern experience. The green beans signify your college degree(s).

I love to create a résumé that has a strong foundation of work experience and professional accomplishments enhanced by a college degree or two. On the other hand, it is tough to market an individual who has little to offer other than a recently earned college degree. It is unfortunate that so many college students and recent graduates thought for so long that their degrees or advanced degrees would drastically improve their careers.

I say this because my résumé used to consist primarily of green beans. I had believed for years that my college degree was just what I needed to get ahead. I expected to be recognized and promoted because of it. Needless to say, I was wrong. No one seemed to care that I graduated *magna cum laude* and worked full time while attending school full time (and year round). No one seemed to care that I had gone three years without a vacation or suffered through a managerial accounting course in the summer. Employers needed to know that I could do the job, and grades just do not prove this by themselves!

If you are in college, you probably know that you get out of it what you put into it. Grades are important, of course, but please do not let them be your only priority. Also watch where you are working during school. If you do not want to work during school, find some time to do some meaningful volunteer work. If you want or need to work during school, look for something related and worthwhile. It does not have to be your dream career, but it will add dimension to your résumé.

If you are doing a job that you feel is worthless to your career advancement, there is hope. First of all, as a résumé writer, I have been able to reveal the responsibility and difficulty of even the most seemingly menial positions. However, if you are an intern taking inventory of the supply cabinet, run. Get out now, and find an internship that will actually teach you something! Do not let any organization take advantage of you.

Designer Degrees

When I was attending college, there were some classes that I found extremely useful and others I thought were a waste of time. I am positive that anyone who has attended college can relate with that.

In the future, I believe that more and more schools are going to offer personalized degree programs. I am very excited about this because this means students will be more in control. People will graduate with a smorgasbord of education, highly specialized or somewhere in between.

Stanford University, for example, will offer custom classes for its MBA students in the fall of 2007. Students are coming from increasingly diverse backgrounds; therefore, some are completely overwhelmed while others are bored and unchallenged by the material in required classes.

Soon students will be able to enroll in classes at standard, intermediate and "challenge" levels (Alsop, 2006). Pair this customized education with related work experience, and I believe graduates will be better able to market themselves to prospective employers.

Actions You Can Take

I encourage you to plan, research and identify trends. Consider your options, and make informed decisions. People today are more open to career change than ever before. So no matter your age, if you are not fulfilled by your current position, start researching other possibilities. At the risk of tooting my own horn, find a career coach. Please notice that I did not say "counselor." If anything about your career coach sounds like counseling, something is wrong. Coaching is more future-oriented, and it may help you come up with options that you never considered before.

Just like customers cannot buy from me if they do not know I exist, you cannot consider a career path if you do not know it exists. This is yet another example of the Internet's usefulness. Faster, greater amounts of information lead to quicker, more informed decisions.

Global Reach

I believe that taking a foreign language should be a requirement in junior high and high school instead of just an option. Learn one in college or take courses outside of work. This simply makes you more marketable, and who does not want that? As more businesses expand globally, so must individuals. If you only worry about what is in your backyard, you will find yourself extremely limited, especially when it comes to finding a satisfying career. If you disagree with the changes you see happening, the worst thing you can do is ignore them and hope they go away.

Immigration is currently a controversial issue in the US, and I expect it to remain this way for some time. I am not implying that English should *not* be the official language, and

I am not saying that we should allow our culture to change as a result of allowing large numbers of immigrants to come to our country legally or illegally. I am simply saying that as prospective employers make themselves more competitive, so should you. You risk not being able to find a fulfilling career.

Job You Deserve is a perfect example of this. The résumé writing industry is still fairly new in English-speaking countries such as the US, Australia and Canada. But think of all of the untapped markets! There are millions of people in India and China who want very badly to work in the US. Language barriers are the first reasons we are hesitant to advertise in these countries. One of my New Year's resolutions for 2006 was to learn Chinese. I am still working on my unfinished project of learning Spanish. But with time, perhaps even the résumé industry and the recruiting industry can benefit from global expansion.

I acknowledge that the US is not the only country with the labor issues described in this chapter. Each country has its own challenges. The fact that other countries are rapidly developing and aggressive recruiters from other countries have their eye on top talent in the US could be good for job seekers because they will have more options. It is fun to consider your options! If living in another country will require you to learn another language, do it. Even if you never relocate, you will have more to offer an employer in the US, which most likely does business in other countries.

Why Résumés Will Never Die

I recently heard someone say that eventually blogs will replace résumés. While networking is still the best way to get a job, you need a résumé that accurately communicates your value.

According to Dictionary.com (2006), a résumé is a summary. It is also defined as "a brief written account of personal, educational, and professional qualifications and experience, as that prepared by an applicant for a job." You need a résumé because it is nearly impossible to sum up *all* of your qualifications in a conversation or an email. Before a personal interview, most employers would like to have something on which to base their questions.

Even if you were referred by a top performing employee, it is good to have a summary of your most notable achievements. When talking to a car dealer, are you going to remember all of the car's features without taking home a brochure or looking at the Web site? It is always a good idea to have a sales brochure to entice readers to want to learn more about you.

The Moral of the Story

This is a good time to be a B player who possesses a unique blend of skills and talents. Whether you are an A or a B, continue to manage your career like a CEO. What is next? Even if business is great, how will you maintain your edge? Would you like to do business in another country? How will you accomplish this? What is your plan?

Continuously network and improve yourself, and you should have no problem finding a fulfilling career.

I hope this book has been inspirational. At the very least, I hope it has been thought provoking. Let me leave you with a quote from an article by recruiter Dr. John Sullivan (2006) that I found very inspirational. Best of luck with your next job search campaign!

"…unlike a military raid, recruiters don't take hostages, they simply offer better opportunities for potential candidates to consider. Employees are not owned; they choose what is best for themselves and their families. If they opt to take advantage of a new opportunity, the shame should not be upon the recruiter, but rather on the former employer for 'taking them for granted and not insuring that the best opportunity was being delivered!'"

References

Alsop, R. (2006, October 10). Stanford offers custom classes for its students. *The Wall Street Journal*, p. B8.

Burt, Erin. (2006). *Top Ten Hottest Jobs.* Retrieved October 10, 2006 from http://www.kiplinger.com/personalfinance/columns/starting/archive/2006/st0907.htm

Dictionary.com. (2006). *8 results for: résumé.* Retrieved October 2, 2006 from http://dictionary.reference.com/browse/résumé

Finder, Alan. (2006). *For Some, Online Persona Undermines a Résumé.*
Retrieved October 2, 2006 from http://www.nytimes.com/2006/06/11/us/11recruit.html?ei=5090&en=ddfbe1e3b386090b&ex=1307678400&partner=rssuserland&emc=rss&pagewanted=all

Mattonen, Karen. (n.d.). *Candidate Rights in the Recruiting Process.*
Retrieved September 21, 2006 from http://www.acssearch.com/candidaterights/

QuietAgent.com (2006). Retrieved October 15, 2006 from http://www.quietagent.com

Sullivan, John. (2006). *How Kevin Bacon Can Help You Recruit No-Cost Referrals.*
Retrieved September 26, 2006, from http://www.ere.net/articles/db/BCD3F629EBC74A23A3369D2BDF29D617.asp

Sullivan, John. (2006). *A Profile of the World's Most Aggressive Recruiter, Part 1.*
Retrieved October 5, 2006 from http://www.ere.net/articles/db/9DC33DE7510D2C9DFB302DF416941AE0.asp

Sullivan, John. (2006). *Recruiting at Bars and Other Places Prospects Gather.*
Retrieved September 26, 2006 from http://www.ere.net/articles/db/8FFA6D54FA1C4843AE276BC1DEFE9CED.asp.

The Princeton Review. (n.d.). *Top 10 Most Popular College Majors.*
Retrieved October 10, 2006 from http://www.
princetonreview.com/college/research/articles/majors/
popular.asp

978-0-595-41896-1
0-595-41896-1

www.ingramcontent.com/pod-product-compliance
Lightning Source LLC
Chambersburg PA
CBHW021023180526
45163CB00005B/2091